21 Days

Jakoby Andrew

Presentation by *BookLeaf Publishing*

Web: www.bookleafpub.com

E-mail: info@bookleafpub.com

ISBN: 9789357745130

First edition 2023

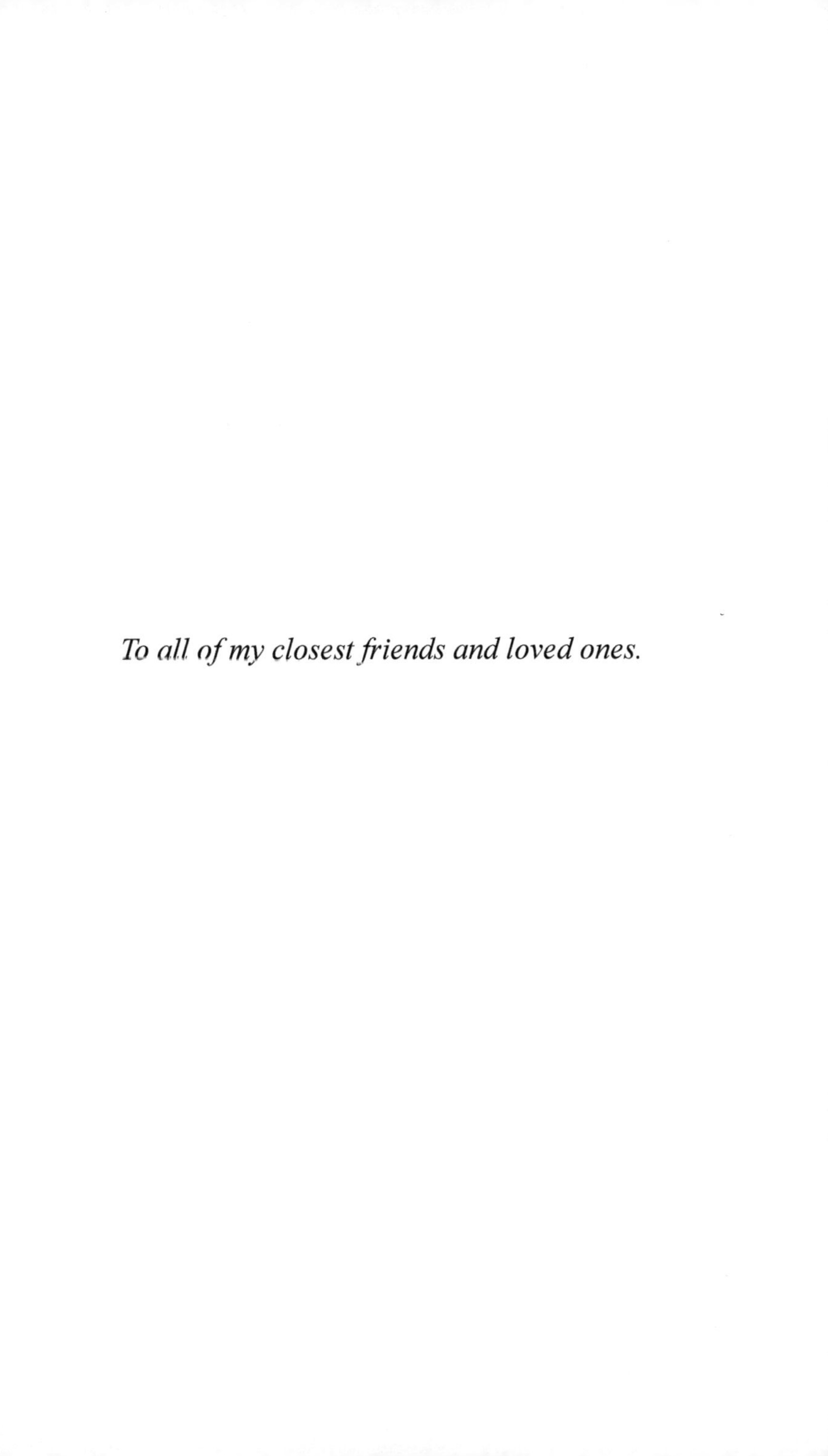

To all of my closest friends and loved ones.

PREFACE

I decided to write this preface after "17: When i was yours" simply because I covered a lot of ground in my personal life these last two and half weeks.

When I set out to do this challenge initially, I aimed to let the muse come out in any raw form that it could, and did my best to capture the thoughts and feelings it wanted me to express.

But what I didn't realize (which I think is explicitly obvious) was the profound effect that love in it's forms has on me. With "When i was yours", I chose the lower case "i" as means of a loss of identity, one I gave away in my last relationship I felt true love in. It ends with the uppercase "I" as the realization of that time in my life finally made sense. A difficult conversation with a close friend took place before I wrote it and something had triggered me, thrusting me back into that headspace. After spending time with loved ones in the days during this challenge, there were many more triggers I hadn't been completely aware of that I'm sure I haven't seen the last of.

But being able to feel the confidence to say "yeah, this is how I feel, this is what I want to say, this is what I want to write" and not feel the abject fear of scrutiny from those who've hurt me (and trust me, I know I've hurt them too), has been freeing. This catharsis is not understated in my mind as love itself has often been a negative aspect of my life, a plague that turned my thoughts toxic and bled into my friendships and relationships.

I feel the need to address this now because I know I haven't seen the last of this trauma and it's likely to return at any given time. But the slight smile that makes me giggle has me realizing I've made incredible progress. Before, my words were filled with hate and blame, often directed at myself and how terribly I viewed myself. I'd flip it towards the others and blame them too when I felt like it was their fault. It's like I finally feel aware of how important of a step this is for me. Why blame each other when maybe all we have to do is figure out what's causing these feelings? Friends and loved ones always tell me "you care about others more than you care about yourself" and I just immediately shut them down since I thought it was the way I needed to live.

But strangely, knowing how I've hurt others and being able to say out loud "I was treated terribly too", and actually realize what effect it has on my life (and subsequent relationships), gives me immense hope. I know there's still a ton of progress to be made, and the memories of those times likely aren't going to go away as easily as I hope they would.

And a friend of mine just texted me as I'm writing this saying, "it's like figuring out a sickness you have, so now you know how to treat it." That's exactly how it feels. To objectively say in "When i was yours" that it's been "Years later and it's still just as fresh" makes me understand how the trauma of love has been poisoning me. Even in "6: Unspoken" I felt that immense fear and anxiety that love brings. I wasn't sure how to contextualize, or maybe, internalize the difference between love and abuse that day. Instead, I wrote my feelings out as if someone had left me heart broken because I felt like they didn't love me.

Something feels different now though. It's pretty obvious I feel better, and I can confidently say this challenge has been exactly what I've needed. I know this is just another step towards the goals I've set out to accomplish, I just had no idea that the phrase "I was your house husband" would clear up so much of my problems with love and that time of my life (*shrug emoji* and an "lol" for good measure).

I hope that this serves as a preface, I mean, I'm just being myself here. Thank you so much for taking the time to experience my writing, and I hope that if there's anything keeping you in the dark or plaguing you, that you can figure it out too, and be honest with yourself and others. I sincerely send my love to all those who stumble upon this and leave you with my favorite thing to say:

Find solace; there is safety in numbers.

- Jakoby

1: Winds of Change

A western wind blows.
Chaotically, throes of dust
sting my fluttering eyes.
"Seventy miles per hour!"
Spoken softly, sour tastes of rust
fill my palette made of sighs.
Breathing heavily at time passing.
Changed heart trespassing with lust
and the wind swallows all my cries.
The city throws it's metal side to side.
Alive, yet inside, currents of my mind
focus solely on this lovesick rise.
Tastes of blood from bleeding heart
carries part of me far from trust,
and unsure, is this another demise?
To give my love is to trust the wind.
Ashamed, a sin, left full of disgust.
And away my heart goes, there it flies.

For a moment I hadn't heard what you said,
but the wind stopped and I patiently thought,
the taste of blood from love's bite subsides,
and I saw you smile, waiting for my response.

2: Sleepless

Exhausted, irritated at the world that's awake.
 Thunderous plane engines,
 blaring television sets,
 muffled laughing shakes
 the very thin walls that fail to stop any sound.
 Blocked lawn sprinklers,
 freezing rain falls,
 old refrigerator hums
 at a tone just lower than the tinnitus.
 Rattling heater groans,
 creaking hallway footsteps,
 roommate's morning shower
 all pile on the soundscape of today's whining.

Even the lovely music playing from the home
speaker
 can't ease the ringing that hasn't let me rest.
 Another few hours spent plugging ears
 just to suffer through why I'm so sleepless.

3: What's it for?

A cyclical cynic once asked me the meaning of
life.
Drink in hand, and a small plastic bag,
they asked me not to judge
as they found peace in
a powdered line done off a phone.
I stumbled through my answer,
nervously watching my friend try to
stay alive.
I stayed quiet,
letting thoughts race feeling like
I enabled another person's
downward spiral.
But they asked me again, and again,
desperately clinging to my words,
looking for an answer
I didn't think I had.
I looked back, and breathed a stale truth,
and I told them I'd rather they be here,
alive,
and it didn't matter what happened in this room,
that all I knew
was they asked me to come over,
because they had nowhere safer to go,
and maybe that's what it was all for.

They laughed at me and said thank you,
and for a small momentary second,
we both smiled.

4: Snowstorm

5

A romantic feeling cripples my throat
 Like deep in mountain high, snow covered
trees.
 Breath in scarcity, there's no antidote.
 No begging to breathe, no need to say please,
 Love must be felt true, in ways naturally.
 Like admiration for life frozen still,
 Feeling everything supernaturally.
 In cold silence though, the power of will
 Does not rest in the endless hope for warm.
 Steady crystal cries freeze my tears sweetly,
 Yet remind I've known romantic snowstorm,
 And that love's warmth must be felt completely.
 Trekking through the treeline, I walk alone,
 Carrying a warm beating heart, my own.

5: Night Out

Shimmering iridescent city light
 reflects off rain soaked road ways.
 Headlights blur on the misty windshield,
 already barely visible from the steam of
laughter and smoke.
 Joking about hobbies in the traffic busy avenue,
 talking about the millions of dollars moving up
and down the street.
 In a sleepless city,
 riding to and from a mostly sober night out,
 I felt safe in a car I wasn't driving.

Lights whizzed by,
 imprinted spots flickered on my eyes.
 The thought of leaving this place stuck in my
mind,
 a future not even sure I would come to find,
 and the laughter faded with our goodbyes.
 Another place, and another time,
 I might have questioned why
 an uncommon rainy night was
 what it meant to be alive.

6: Unspoken

Clouds parted ways
  like glass window panes.
 Frigid wind stays,
  bedsheets filled with stains.
 We shared our tears,
  you swallowed your voice.
 Scared to share fears
  and I had no choice.
 I listened close,
  you said nothing back.
 I took a dose,
  an insomniac.
 Did you refuse
  while we saw the sky?
 What's your excuse,
  leaving me to cry?
 I stared alone,
  starry night sees this.

I've always known
 I'd go with no kiss.
 You smiled nervous,
  now I can't forget.
 Provide service,
  just your silhouette.

My shadow knows
 the truth that's behind.
Numbing wind blows,
 I'm losing my mind.
You said goodbye,
 I said I love you.
Silent, your eye,
 questioning what's true.
I left and fled
 with a heart broken.
Left what I bled
 in words unspoken.

7: Hold onto

9

Blood rush, head rush, fast,
Infatuation between
Tired, kindly smiling.
Future's presence near,
Separation physically,
In heart and mind, here.
Patient breathless laughs
Moving softly, carefully,
Temperate caress
Ebbing blood flow moves
Dissipating time slowly.
Spent holding onto,
Beating hearts faster.
Eyes dart, confusion sets in,
Only this matters.

8: Scared

Pour a drink,
 numb the senses that taste apple carbonation,
 distort the tongue and become chlorine.
 Traumatic flavor,
 drowning in the past fear where life ended,
 before it began.
 Weightless, terrified, belly filled with pool
water.
 Sit here now,
 mix the sedation, and damn the hands that can't
write tonight.

Come back later to see how scared I am.
Scared to let life it's time.
To grow passed the past,
 the old roots and stems must be unearthed.
Cut off the head of the voice
 screaming so loud that death was desirable.
Drink it numb, pop it too,
But I'll wake tomorrow and everything still
exists.
Wonder how this existentialism will be lost on
any of those who read me.
But smile knowing simply,
Life goes on.

The past has passed me by.
The future has nothing but potential.
And the present sits with me writing this
now.

9: Senseless Obsession

Drifting away, coursing through empty space.
Ambiguous shifting particles float by,
stardust, they say.
Vibrations forming faces,
vibrations forming voices,
vibrations forming feelings,
vibrations forming endlessness.
Deliberately disassociating
so I may forget your star-born noise.
Glistening infinity echoes blinding light,
reflection of vibrating presence.
That in these pools of sight,
deafening thought shakes the hulls of my mind
and all sound silences all senses.

Vessel made of dust, sensations of vibrations
cause chaos to stir the mind and focus on
Obsession.
Obsessed with the sights of monochromatic
surroundings.
Obsessed with the sounds of silent whispers,
swearing nothingness.
Obsessed with the touch of searing present
tense.

Obsessed with the taste of sour sores from salt
base.
And obsessed with the smell of stale dust
building from isolation.

Drifting away, away from empty space.
Dissatisfied with this form,
but the vibrations never stop
and their sound surrounds me, starting to make
sense.

10: Waste My Time

I don't want to ever waste my time,
 but here I lay, caught in your sublime.
 Stolen heart, no need to report a crime,
 wasting away here, finding words that rhyme.
 Wishful and yet willfully waiting
 to hear you were done with debating.
 And I find no need for contemplating,
 being patient is exhilarating.

Minute hands move seconds off the clock.
Hour hands budge slowly with a tick tock.
Mesmerized by the sound of your knock,
hopeful that this will cure my writer's block.
All my stories' pages have turned blank.
Time wasted in the days I have drank,
and nervous before, my heart it sank.
But you took my mind, I have you to thank.

11: Reminiscent (New Year's Eve)

Sixteen intersecting beams of faint darkness
 cut through the sixteen streams of opal colored
streaks,
 emanating from a dying candle behind crude
glass designed to look crystalized.

The aroma, a nearly lost orange and pear wax.
 Boiled off is the smell the senses recovered
from pandemic infection.
At the very moment of finishing the line before,
the candle succumbed to the beams of darkness.

Now jet black holds onto closet door,
Mother's awake soft red Christmas lights
barrel through the hallway to crack slightly
into the broken spots where the cheap bedroom
door fails to stop it.

Electric light in technicolor rainbows
overstimulate the senses.
The fan blows all air around,
whisking the last oil's breath across the room
into darkness beyond sight.

Mind oh mind, what is there really to be afraid
of here?

No sight or smell or taste or feeling could hear
my mother coughing beyond the rattling of the
fan that may not even act as noise to keep me
asleep.

But my dreams of places beyond here are
dreams of the problems that exist,
 and my sense beyond sleep is just as dulled
from
 this senseless sickness that killed a few million.

I'm surviving this now,
 why be so afraid of the dark?

(12/31/22)

12: I don't care today

I don't care,
Not right now, not for a while.
I can't tell when it started,
Or why it won't stop.
I just don't care.
About anything, anyone, or even my own life.
I put these words down just to keep pace,
Hoping something would break through,
But I just don't care.
If I knew the reason why,
I would care.
If I knew when it would stop,
I would care.
But not right now, not for a while.
Even the beauty of the sky,
Or the wonders of the world,
Or the shining of her eyes,
I just don't care.
No one to give me advice,
I won't listen.
No one to hold me close,
I won't feel it.
No one to take my focus,
I won't see it.
And if all my senses were somehow clear,

And my mind could think about anything at all,
And if this depression could somehow bring a
smile,
And if I could really find safety in numbers,
I would care.

But now?
Right here?
On this page?
I don't care,

But I wish I did.

13: Light and Dark

The light goes out,
  the darkness rests still
  in this room only voiced
  by a mechanical whirring.
 This fight is about
  finding the power in will,
  and no matter the choice,
  life keeps on stirring.
 Varying greys outline the walls,
  faint blues reflect off electric clocks,
  metallic box humming reflects
  pale light off the loudest thing in here.
 In rooms darker, subject to internal falls,
  found with doors closed and metal locks,
  that clanking engaging deflected
  the eternal guttural groan of fear.

 In time, my mind, blinded, finds signs, patterns
and designs, that outline the darkness's shine.

 The light fights with that mighty shine, but the
trite delightful of white blinding light takes my
sight.

Forceful coursing thoughts sure to be
distraught, caught me rotten. Decaying, praying
for lessons taught, yet hopeful it would stay.

But often, the light goes away, and I find I'm
still blind in the dark's earshot, hearing, fearing
that this is all for naught.

The light turns back on,
 and the dark doesn't seem so loud.

14: Heat

21

Scorching fire burns fingertips.
 Steadily shaking, anxious.
 Pulled tight, slight kiss on the lips,
 readily waiting for more.
 Digging nails into the flesh,
 never wanting anything.
 Past's scars begin to refresh,
 sever the touch of before.
 Enthralled in present passions,
 insides boiling nervously.
 Covered with all her fashions,
 tides of heat waves fill my core.
 Clutching on, wrapped up tighter,
 staying a second longer.
 Warmth grips, body feels lighter,
 praying for this evermore.

Letting go, but not wanting to,
 the cold alone once filled up the room.
 But after holding onto you,
 icy thoughts thaw from this lovers' bloom.

15: Nothing I can do

Chemical chaos,
 A physical dissonance
 Between this romance.
 A sensual touch
 Invites a whirlwind headspace
 Terrifying me.
 Holding on tightly
 Then pulled closer, face to face,
 And I see your love.
 We both know what's wrong.
 Cannot change who we've become,
 But my love won't stop.
 Endure to feel this,
 And love truly, but I know
 Peace may never come.

16: Piano Sound

23

The muse has finally left.
The dim television,
in multicolored luminescence,
fills the shadows of white keys
with black trimmings.
Collect the dust,
emanate no sound,
and mute the feeling
speakers once spoke,
filled with particles
that burn the eyes.
Heavy lids close,
catching a glimpse of notes
not yet played,
and the wonder of possibilities
echoes a similar sound,
one too fill with dust.

17: When i was yours

Clean the dishes, do the laundry,
 Wipe the floors, pay your rent.
Do what you want,
Do what you ask,
Don't have a single thought,
Unless you want to fight.
Pay me in conditions,
Fuck me when i've done it all,
But don't i dare fall in love,
You don't pay me for that.
Wait for hours because you asked,
And make sure to stay by the phone.
Listen to your stories, watch all of your shows,
And don't do anything without permission.
Sleep alone in the living room,
And keep quiet at night,
You're trying to sleep.
Don't cry so loud,
Don't tell a soul about this,
Don't say anything, we're so fine,
And never question what you say
Because i'm the one who does it all wrong.

Be sure to say how bad i was,
Say it to all my friends,
And tell me what i should've done better,

And fuck me up so badly now,
i'm not really sure how to love.
Leave me with a broken heart,
And tell me to pick up the pieces,
But be sure to take some with you too,
i wouldn't want to put this all on you.
Tell me about how much better life is,
And all the friends you've made,
And be sure to let me know,
How it's all my own fault.

i let this happen, but to what extent?

Years later and it's still just as fresh.
New love comes around,
i shudder and shy away so quickly,
And i feel you breathing on my neck.
Even when i have to wait,
It's like i'm waiting for you,
Alone in a desolate room,
Just to hear your words of hate.
Try to explain and fail to understand
How deep the scar tissue goes,
And remember so vividly
That day when i refused your hand.
The anger you felt when i tried to stand,
You kicked in my bad knee,
But i had no choice those days when

I was your house husband.

18: Day One

I told a loved one how I felt,
 melting mindset at the thought of the past,
  lasting trauma brought on from captivity.
 Activity shut down, I'd be a husk of myself.
  Hell brought on by dusk, the morning,
 a warning I'd have to wake to the truth,
  proof I was someone else before.

They saw me, trying, and told me so,
 knowing who I am now, and what I feel.
  Reality felt like it made it here today,
 saying "have a little fun before the break,
  take your time and cherish what you spend."
 Pretending once, thoughts didn't bother me,
  seeing them smile when I smiled more.

An old song came up, loudly it played,
 stayed present and I began singing,
  bringing a joy I hadn't felt from it since,
 wincing but not losing my mind,
  finding enjoyment when I thought it gone,
 dawning on me that yesterday has passed,
  lasting far longer, buried deep in my core.

Finally coming to, I felt what was gripping,

ripping me from right now, falling backwards
 towards the memories I couldn't sever,
forever stuck in a room, crying alone,
 knowing it wouldn't last, I just had to run.
 Gunning towards everyone quicker,
 sicker than ever at the truth of a slamming
door,

but I woke up and felt how excited I got,
brought on by some love, some fun, on this
 day one.

19: Yesterday

Exhaustion yet again clenched upon my body.
 Found a drive, a desire, a god-fearing fire,
 and walked a few miles to see the stage.
 One-note singing beckoned through the muted
doors,
 ears began to ring, and a pitch black theater
called.
 I heard it calmly, tiredly I slumped in my seat.
 Women sang songs in the same tone.
 Strings, keys, and beats filled this dark room,
 and for a few hours all I could think of was how
tired I was.

 Cleaning a room and watching the hour hands
tick upwards,
 I felt love dueling fear.
 You left me filled with hope, and I awoke,
 tremendously happy to hold you so close.
 Through a bedridden rest, a drained loneliness,
 I accomplished everything I set out for
yesterday.
 And though you have left,
 and the singing barely left me impressed,
 I know why I had to wake up today.

20: Today

Glitz, gold, and glamour, millions of eyes,
A stage burning, with heart and mind.
Gratefully listening, a breath alive,
Soul ablaze, a flame deep inside.
Doubt echoes, its fearsome quake,
The future bellows, while the past it aches.
Tears warming, my sight awake,
Cannot give up now, for Everything's sake.

21

On the last day, chaotic winds have finally left
me.
 Solemnly escaping, the words now have
nothing to say.
 For today, my mind away, and there's nothing
special to see.
 A complex shaping of feelings that always
seems to stay.
 And now, thoughts they stray, grasping at a
muse once free,
 I feel my throat taping, laced with a new game I
must play.

 A future brings another challenge, one that must
go,
 forward, towards blue skies, and sharp wind
that stings,
 And a bird sings, signalling what I already
know.
 Seasons change and old lies choked me with
their strings,
 I breathe, spread wings, and fly into the wind
that blows.
 Those old cries always seem to rise with
Spring's sunrise

and sunshine dried my skin and colors filled the
space.
 In emeralds, sky blues, metallic grays, a
returning pallette tried
 to bring life to what died any time I thought of
your face.
 But those winter days warmed and the snow
then cried
 and went silent, but pried my breath, froze it
cold, and left without a trace.
 Now, wind and I alive, it sways, and I find what
I lost

from the days I thought I died.